PRENTICE HALL

WORLD GEOGRAPHY
BUILDING A GLOBAL PERSPECTIVE

Guided Reading and Review Workbook

Needham, Massachusetts
Upper Saddle River, New Jersey
Glenview, Illinois

ISBN 0-13-067870-8

3 4 5 6 7 8 9 10   06 05 04 03

Table of Contents

Success in social studies comes from doing three things well—reading, testing, and writing. The following pages present strategies to help you read for meaning, understand test questions, and write well.

Reading for Meaning

Do you have trouble remembering what you read? Here are some tips from experts that will improve your ability to recall and understand what you read:

BEFORE YOU READ

Preview the text to identify important information.
Like watching the coming attractions at a movie theater, previewing the text helps you know what to expect. Study the questions and strategies below to learn how to preview what you read.

Ask yourself these questions:	Use these strategies to find the answers:
• What is the text about?	Read the headings, subheadings, and captions. Study the photos, maps, tables, or graphs.
• What do I already know about the topic?	Read the questions at the end of the text to see if you can answer any of them.
• What is the purpose of the text?	Turn the headings into *who, what, when, where, why,* or *how* questions. This will help you decide if the text compares things, tells a chain of events, or explains causes and effects.

Organize information in a way that helps you see meaningful connections or relationships.

Taking notes as you read will improve your understanding. Use graphic organizers like the ones below to record the information you read. Study these descriptions and examples to learn how to create each type of organizer.

Sequencing

A **flowchart** helps you see how one event led to another. It can also display the steps in a process.

Use a flowchart if the text—
- tells about a chain of events.
- explains a method of doing something.

TIP▶ List the events or steps in order.

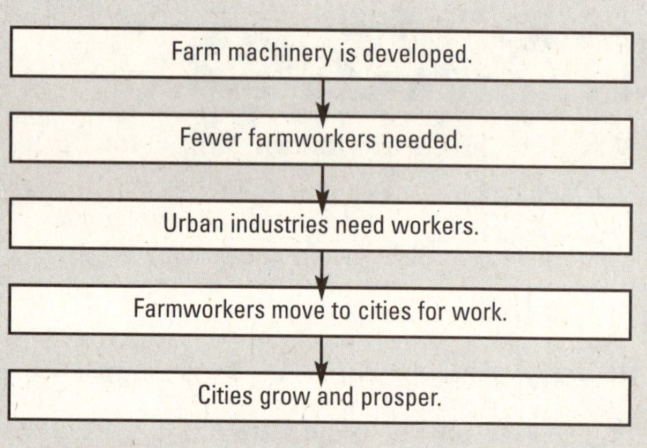

Comparing and Contrasting

A **Venn diagram** displays similarities and differences.

Use a Venn diagram if the text—
- compares and contrasts two individuals, groups, places, things, or events.

TIP▶ Label the outside section of each circle and list differences.
Label the shared section and list similarities.

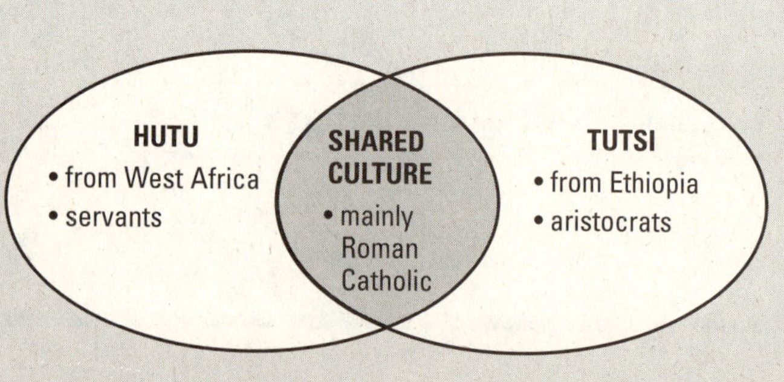

Categorizing Information

A **chart** organizes information in categories.

Use a chart if the text—
- lists similar facts about several places or things.
- presents characteristics of different groups.

TIP▶ Write an appropriate heading for each column in the chart to identify its category.

COUNTRY	FORM OF GOVERNMENT	ECONOMY
Cuba	communist dictatorship	command economy
Puerto Rico	democracy	free enterprise system

Identifying Main Ideas and Details

A **concept web** helps you understand relationships among ideas.

Use a concept web if the text—
- provides examples to support a main idea.
- links several ideas to a main topic.

TIP▶ Write the main idea in the largest circle. Write details in smaller circles and draw lines to show relationships.

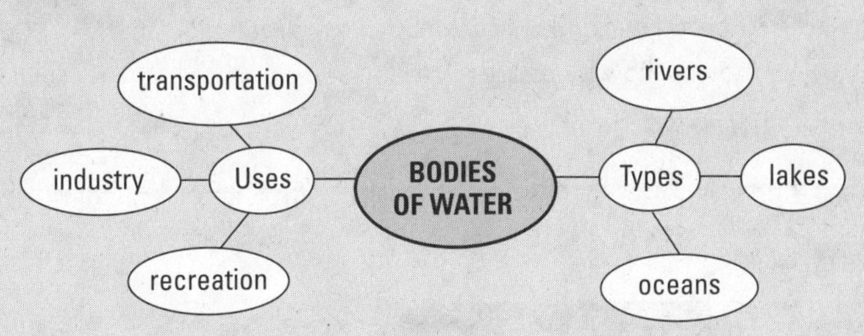

An **outline** provides an overview, or a kind of blueprint for reading.

Use an outline to organize ideas—
- according to their importance.
- according to the order in which they are presented.

TIP▶ Use Roman numerals for main ideas, capital letters for secondary ideas, and Arabic numerals for supporting details.

I. Differences Between the North and the South
   A. Views on slavery
      1. Northern abolitionists
      2. Southern slave owners
   B. Economies
      1. Northern manufacturing
      2. Southern agriculture

A **cause-and-effect** diagram shows the relationship between what happened (effect) and the reason why it happened (cause).

Use a cause-and-effect chart if the text—
- lists one or more causes for an event.
- lists one or more results of an event.

TIP▶ Label causes and effects. Draw arrows to indicate how ideas are related.

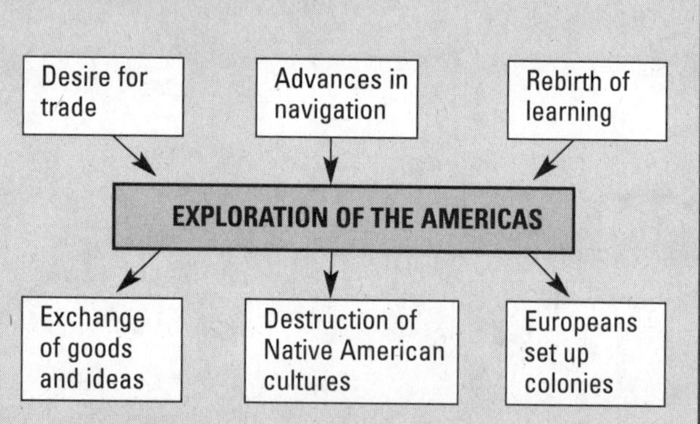

AFTER YOU READ

Test yourself to find out what you learned from reading the text.

Go back to the questions you asked yourself before you read the text. You should be able to give more complete answers to these questions:
- What is the text about?
- What is the purpose of the text?

You should also be able to make connections between the new information you learned from the text and what you already knew about the topic.

Study your graphic organizer. Use this information as the *answers*. Make up a meaningful *question* about each piece of information.

Taking Tests

Do you panic at the thought of taking a standardized test?
Here are some tips that most test developers recommend to
help you achieve good scores.

MULTIPLE-CHOICE QUESTIONS

**Read each part of a multiple-choice question to make sure you
understand what is being asked.**

Many tests are made up of multiple-choice questions. Some multiple-choice
items are **direct questions.** They are complete sentences followed by possible
answers, called distractors.

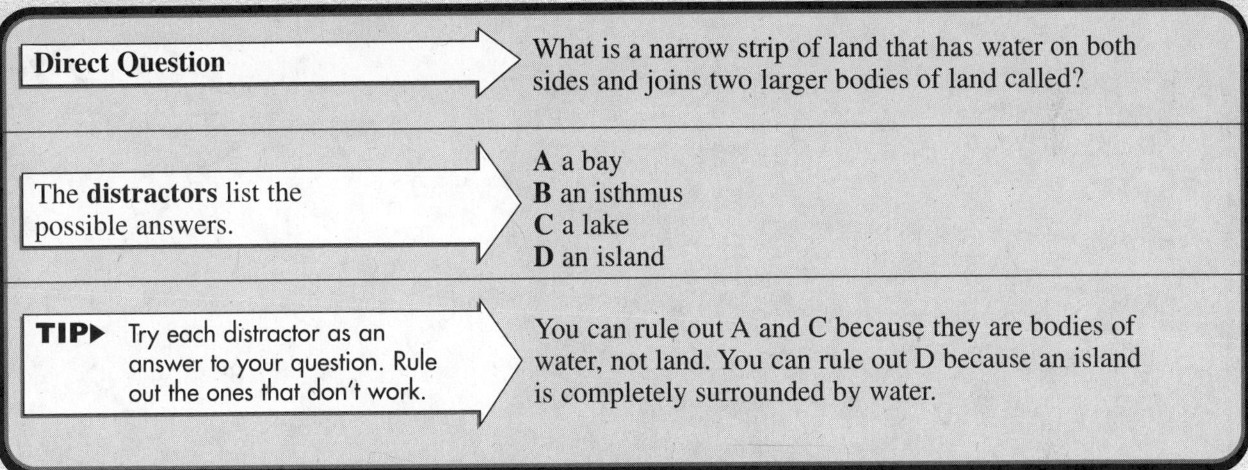

Other multiple-choice questions are **incomplete sentences** that you are to
finish. They are followed by possible answers.

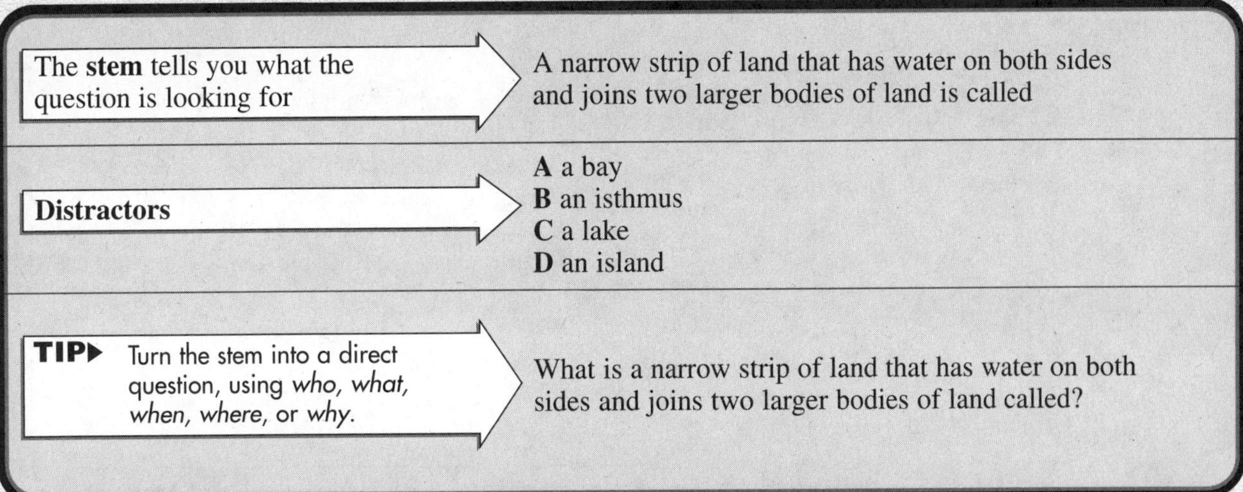

WHAT'S BEING TESTED?

Identify the type of question you are being asked.

Social studies tests often ask questions that involve reading comprehension. Other questions may require you to gather or interpret information from a map, graph, or chart. The following strategies will help you answer different kinds of questions.

Reading Comprehension Questions

What to do:

How to do it:

1. Determine the content and organization of the selection.

Read the **title.** Skim the selection. Look for key words that indicate time, cause-and-effect, or comparison.

2. Analyze the questions.
Do they ask you to *recall facts?*

Look for **key words** in the stem:
According to the selection . . .
The selection states that . . .

Do they ask you to *make judgments?*

The main idea of the selection is . . .
The author would likely agree that . . .

3. Read the selection.

Read quickly. Keep the questions in mind.

4. Answer the questions.

Try out each distractor and choose the best answer. Refer back to the selection if necessary.

Example:
A Region of Diversity The Khmer empire was one of many kingdoms in Southeast Asia. Unlike the Khmer empire, however, the other kingdoms were small because Southeast Asia's mountains kept people protected and apart. People had little contact with those who lived outside their own valley.

Why were most kingdoms in Southeast Asia small?
A disease killed many people
B lack of food
C climate was too hot
D mountains kept people apart

TIP▶ The key word because tells why the kingdoms were small.
(The correct answer is D.)

Map Questions

What to do:	**How to do it:**
1. Determine what kind of information is presented on the map.	Read the map **title.** It will indicate the purpose of the map. Study the **map key.** It will explain the symbols used on the map. Look at the **scale.** It will help you calculate distance between places on the map.
2. Read the question. Determine which component on the map will help you find the answer.	Look for **key words** in the stem. About <u>how far</u> . . . [use the scale] <u>What crops</u> were grown in . . . [use the map key]
3. Look at the map and answer the question in your own words.	Do not read the distractors yet.
4. Choose the best answer.	Decide which distractor agrees with the answer you determined from the map.

Eastern Europe: Language Groups

In which of these countries are Thraco-Illyrian languages spoken?

A Romania
B Albania
C Hungary
D Lithuania

TIP▶ Read the labels and the key to understand the map.
(The correct answer is B.)

What to do:

1. Determine the purpose of the graph.

2. Determine what information on the graph will help you find the answer.

3. Choose the best answer.

How to do it:

Read the graph **title.** It indicates what the graph represents.

Read the **labels** on the graph or on the key. They tell the units of measurement used by the graph.

Decide which distractor agrees with the answer you determined from the graph.

Example

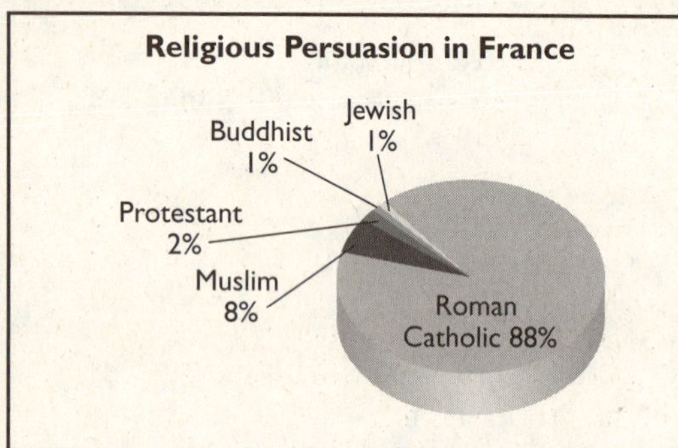

A **Circle graph** shows the relationship of parts to the whole in terms of percentages.

After Roman Catholics, the next largest religious population in France is
A Buddhist   **C** Jewish
B Protestant   **D** Muslim

TIP▶ Compare the percentages listed in the labels. (The correct answer is D.)

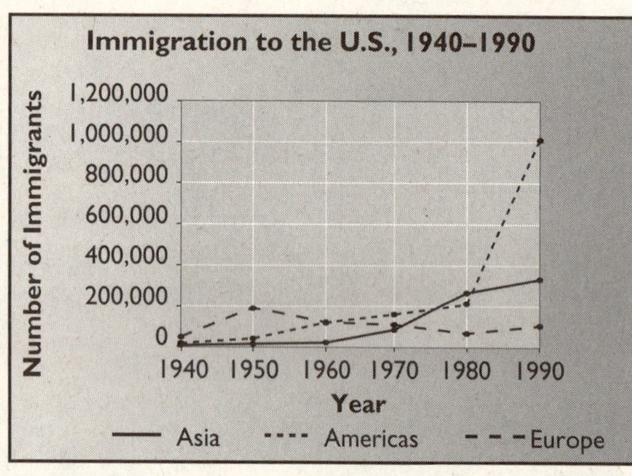

A **line graph** shows a pattern or change over time by the direction of the line.

Between 1980 and 1990, immigration to the U.S. from the Americas
A decreased a little   **C** stayed about the same
B increased greatly   **D** increased a little

TIP▶ Compare the vertical distance between the two correct points on the line graph. (The correct answer is B.)

A **bar graph** compares differences in quantity by showing bars of different lengths.

Saudi Arabia produces about how many more billion of barrels of oil a year than Iran?
A 5 million   **C** 15 million
B 10 million   **D** 20 million

TIP▶ Compare the heights of the bars to find the difference. (The correct answer is B.)

Writing for Social Studies

When you face a writing assignment, do you think, "How will I ever get through this?" Here are some tips to guide you through any writing project from start to finish.

THE WRITING PROCESS

Follow each step of the writing process to communicate effectively.

Step 1. Prewrite

- Establish the purpose.
- Define the topic.
- Determine the audience.
- Gather details.

Step 2. Draft

- Organize information logically in an outline or graphic organizer.
- Write an introduction, body, and conclusion.
- State main ideas clearly.
- Include relevant details to support your ideas.

Step 3. Revise

- Edit for clarity of ideas and elaboration.

Step 4. Proofread

- Correct any errors in spelling, grammar, and punctuation.

Step 5. Publish and Present

- Copy text neatly by hand, or use a typewriter or word processor.
- Illustrate as needed.
- Create a cover, if appropriate.

TYPES OF WRITING FOR SOCIAL STUDIES

Identify the purpose for your writing.

Each type of writing assignment has a specific purpose, and each purpose needs a different plan for development. The following descriptions and examples will help you identify the three purposes for social studies writing. The lists of steps will help you plan your writing.

Writing to Inform

Purpose: to present facts or ideas

Example

During the 1960s, research indicated the dangers of the insecticide DDT. It killed insects but also had long-term effects. When birds and fish ate poisoned insects, DDT built up in their fatty tissue. The poison also showed up in human beings who ate birds and fish contaminated by DDT.

TIP▶ Look for these **key terms** in the assignment: explain, describe, report, narrate

How to get started:
- Determine the topic you will write about.
- Write a topic sentence that tells the main idea.
- List all the ideas you can think of that are related to the topic.
- Arrange the ideas in logical order.

Writing to Persuade

Purpose: to influence someone

Example

Teaching computer skills in the classroom uses time that could be spent teaching students how to think for themselves or how to interact with others. Students who can reason well, express themselves clearly, and get along with other people will be better prepared for life than those who can use a computer.

TIP▶ Look for these **key terms** in the assignment: convince, argue, request

How to get started:
- Make sure you understand the problem or issue clearly.
- Determine your position.
- List evidence to support your arguments.
- Predict opposing views.
- List evidence you can use to overcome the opposing arguments.

Writing to Provide Historical Interpretations

Purpose: to present the perspective of someone in a different era

Example

The crossing took a week, but the steamship voyage was hard. We were cramped in steerage with hundreds of others. At last we saw the huge statue of the lady with the torch. In the reception center, my mother held my hand while the doctor examined me. Then, my father showed our papers to the official, and we collected our bags. I was scared as we headed off to find a home in our new country.

TIP▶ Look for these **key terms** in the assignment: go back in time, create, suppose that, if you were

How to get started:
- Study the events or issues of the time period you will write about.
- Consider how these events or issues might have affected different people at the time.
- Choose a person whose views you would like to present.
- Identify the thoughts and feelings this person might have experienced.

RESEARCH FOR WRITING

Follow each step of the writing process to communicate effectively.

After you have identified the purpose for your writing, you may need to do research. The following steps will help you plan, gather, organize, and present information.

Step 1. Ask Questions

Ask yourself questions to help guide your research.	What do I already know about the topic? What do I want to find out about the topic?

Step 2. Acquire Information

Locate and use appropriate sources of information about the topic.	Library Internet search Interviews
Take notes.	Follow accepted format for listing sources.

Step 3. Analyze Information

Evaluate the information you find.	Is it relevant to the topic? Is it up-to-date? Is it accurate? Is the writer an authority on the topic? Is there any bias?

Step 4. Use Information

Answer your research questions with the information you have found. (You may find that you need to do more research.)	Do I have all the information I need?
Organize your information into the main points you want to make. Identify supporting details.	Arrange ideas in outline form or in a graphic organizer.

Step 5. Communicate What You've Learned

Review the purpose for your writing and choose an appropriate way to present the information.	**Purpose**	**Presentation**
	inform	formal paper, documentary, multimedia
	persuade	essay, letter to the editor, speech
	interpret	journal, newspaper account, drama
Draft and revise your writing, and then evaluate it.	Use a rubric for self-evaluation.	

EVALUATING YOUR WRITING

Use the following rubric to help you evaluate your writing.

	Excellent	Good	Acceptable	Unacceptable
Purpose	Achieves purpose—to inform, persuade, or provide historical interpretation—very well	Informs, persuades, or provides historical interpretation reasonably well	Reader cannot easily tell if the purpose is to inform, persuade, or provide historical interpretation	Lacks purpose
Organization	Develops ideas in a very clear and logical way	Presents ideas in a reasonably well-organized way	Reader has difficulty following the organization	Lacks organization
Elaboration	Explains all ideas with facts and details	Explains most ideas with facts and details	Includes some supporting facts and details	Lacks supporting details
Use of Language	Uses excellent vocabulary and sentence structure with no errors in spelling, grammar, or punctuation	Uses good vocabulary and sentence structure with very few errors in spelling, grammar, or punctuation	Includes some errors in grammar, punctuation, and spelling	Includes many errors in grammar, punctuation, and spelling

Section 1 Guided Reading and Review
The Study of Geography

A. As You Read

Directions: As you read Section 1, answer the following questions and complete the chart.

1. What tools do geographers use to understand the world? ______________________

2. What is a geographic concept? _____________________________________

3. List 10 geographic concepts. ______________________________________

   ____

4. What are two ways geographers describe the location of a place? ______________

   ____

5. What does the character of a place consist of? ___________________________

6. What are the three types of regions? _________________________________

7. What is the movement of a place? ___________________________________

   ____

8. What are some examples of negative effects of human-environment interaction?

   ____

B. Reviewing Vocabulary

Directions: Complete each sentence by writing the correct term in the blank.

9. The position of a place on the globe is its _______________ location.

10. The _______________ of a place consists of its physical characteristics and human characteristics.

11. A central place and the surrounding places affected by it make up a(n) _______________ region.

12. _______________ is the study of where people, places, and things are located and how they relate to each other.

13. A viewpoint that is influenced by one's own culture and experience is _______________ .

14. The location of a place compared to other places is its _______________ location.

15. People's feelings and attitudes about an area define a(n) _______________ region.

16. A(n) _______________ uses computer technology to collect, manipulate, analyze, and display data about the earth's surface.

17. An area in which a certain characteristic is found everywhere is a(n) _______________ region.

18. The Equator divides the earth into two halves or _______________ .

Section 2 Guided Reading and Review

Changes Within the Earth

A. As You Read

Directions: As you read Section 2, complete the chart below concerning internal forces of the earth.

Cause	Effect
Molten rock breaks through the earth's surface.	1. _______________
Large, sudden rock movements occur along a fault.	2. _______________
Two plates pull away from each other.	3. _______________
An oceanic plate meets a continental plate.	4. _______________
Two continental plates collide.	5. _______________

B. Reviewing Vocabulary

Directions: Complete each sentence by writing the correct term in the blank.

6. The center of the earth is called the _______________ .

7. A thick layer of rock called the _______________ is around the earth's core.

8. The earth's _______________ is a thin rocky surface.

9. Soil, rocks, landforms, and other surface features make up the _______________ .

10. The _______________ is the layer of air, water, and other substances above the surface of the earth.

11. The water in oceans, lakes, rivers, and under the ground makes up the

     _______________ .

12. The _______________ is the world of plants, animals, and other living things that occupy the land and waters of the planet.

13. _______________ are the large landmasses in the earth's oceans.

14. Landforms are classified by differences in _______________ —that is, differences in elevation.

15. _______________ is a theory that the earth's outer shell is not one piece of rock.

16. The idea that all continents were once a single landmass but are now separate is called

     the _______________ .

17. The _______________ is a circle of volcanic mountains around the Pacific Ocean.

Section 3 Guided Reading and Review

Changes on the Earth's Surface

A. As You Read

Directions: The two categories of external forces that change the earth's surface are shown below. As you read Section 3, fill in the boxes with examples of each.

Weathering	
Mechanical Weathering	**Chemical Weathering**
1. ________________________ ________________________	3. ________________________ ________________________
2. ________________________ ________________________	4. ________________________ ________________________

Erosion		
5. _____________ _____________	6. _____________ _____________	7. _____________ _____________

B. Reviewing Vocabulary

Directions: Read the statements below. If a statement is true, write T in the blank provided. If it is false, write F.

_________ **8.** The process of weathering breaks down rock at or near the earth's surface.

_________ **9.** Mechanical weathering strengthens rocks.

_________ **10.** Chemical weathering cannot alter a rock's chemical makeup.

_________ **11.** Acid rain is a form of mechanical weathering.

_________ **12.** The movement of the earth's weathered materials is known as erosion.

_________ **13.** Moving water carries sediment—small particles of soil, sand, and gravel.

_________ **14.** Windblown deposits of mineral-rich dust and silt are called loess.

_________ **15.** Glaciers are an agent of weathering.

_________ **16.** Rocks and debris left behind by glaciers are called moraines.

Section 1 Guided Reading and Review

Weather and Climate

A. As You Read

Directions: As you read Section 1, complete the chart below. List the aspects of the earth's weather and climate indicated by the descriptions.

Description	Identification
This reflects some heat back into space and traps some heat near the earth.	1. _______________________
This process distributes the heat from the sun around the earth.	2. _______________________
This occurs when cooler air cannot retain all its vapor.	3. _______________________
These features affect surrounding climates because their temperatures are slow to change.	4. _______________________
This is the most common type of precipitation.	5. _______________________

B. Reviewing Vocabulary

Directions: Complete each sentence by writing the correct term in the blank.

6. _______________________ is the condition of the bottom layer of the earth's atmosphere in one place over a short period of time.

7. _______________________ refers to the weather patterns of an area over a long time.

8. The earth spins like a top in a movement called _______________________.

9. The earth orbits the sun, completing one _______________________ in a year.

10. Two seasons are marked by the summer and winter _______________________.

11. The spring and fall seasons are marked by a(n) _______________________.

12. _______________________ is all forms of water that fall on the earth.

13. Air masses are known as _______________________.

14. Climates of interior regions of a landmass, marked by warm or hot summers and cold, snowy winters, are called _______________________.

Section 2 Guided Reading and Review
Ecosystems

A. As You Read

Directions: As you read Section 2, describe the ecosystems by filling in the chart below.

Ecosystem	Climate	Vegetation
Tropical Rain Forest	1. _______	2. _______
Mid-Latitude Forest	3. _______	4. _______
Coniferous Forest	5. _______	6. _______
Tropical Grasslands	7. _______	8. _______
Temperate Grasslands	9. _______	10. _______
Desert	11. _______	12. _______
Tundra	13. _______	14. _______

B. Reviewing Vocabulary

Directions: Read the statements below. If a statement is true, write T in the blank provided. If it is false, write F.

_______ **15.** Deciduous trees shed their leaves during one season, usually autumn.

_______ **16.** Herbivores are animals that eat plants and meat.

_______ **17.** An ecosystem is formed by the interaction of plants, animals, and the physical environment in which they live.

_______ **18.** North America's temperate grasslands are prairies.

_______ **19.** Coniferous forests contain mostly broadleaf trees.

_______ **20.** Permafrost is a layer of soil just below the surface of the tundra that is always frozen.

_______ **21.** A biome is a major type of ecosystem.

_______ **22.** In tundra regions, the temperature is always very warm.

_______ **23.** A savanna is a tropical grassland.

_______ **24.** Carnivores are meat-eating animals.

_______ **25.** Chaparral is a type of grassland.

Section 1 Guided Reading and Review

The Study of Human Geography

A. As You Read

Directions: As you read Section 1, answer the following questions.

1. Why is the population density different in various parts of the world?

2. What are some possible negative effects of world population growth? What are possible positive effects?

3. List four of the elements of culture.

4. How can the movement of a group of people from one country to another cause cultural change?

B. Reviewing Vocabulary

Directions: Match the definitions in Column I with the terms in Column II. Write the correct letter in each blank.

Column I

__________ 5. the number of live births each year per 1,000 people

__________ 6. referring to the countryside

__________ 7. a place where important ideas begin and spread out

__________ 8. the average number of people in a square mile or kilometer

__________ 9. people who leave a country to live elsewhere

__________ 10. occurs when the skills, arts, ideas, habits, and institutions of one culture come in contact with those of another culture

__________ 11. the growth of city population

__________ 12. the beliefs and actions that define a group of people's way of life

__________ 13. the process by which a cultural element is transmitted across some distance from one group or individual to another

__________ 14. people who move into a country

__________ 15. the result of the restriction of a culture from outside cultural influences

Column II

a. immigrants
b. culture
c. urbanization
d. culture hearth
e. rural
f. emigrants
g. population density
h. diffusion
i. cultural convergence
j. birthrate
k. cultural divergence

Section 2 Guided Reading and Review
Political and Economic Systems

A. As You Read

Directions: As you read Section 2, complete the chart below by ranking political or economic systems based upon the characteristic indicated.

Political and Economic Systems	Rankings
Political systems: confederation, federation, unitary system Characteristic: most to least central government authority	1. ______________________ 2. ______________________ 3. ______________________
Political systems: democracy, dictatorship Characteristic: most to least power of citizens	4. ______________________ 5. ______________________
Economic systems: traditional economy, command economy, market economy Characteristic: most to least government control of the economy	6. ______________________ 7. ______________________ 8. ______________________

B. Reviewing Vocabulary

Directions: Read the statements below. If a statement is true, write T in the blank. If it is false, write F.

__________ **9.** Sovereignty refers to the land and water of a country.

__________ **10.** The United States is a democracy and a federation.

__________ **11.** Great Britain is both a confederation and a constitutional monarchy.

__________ **12.** A dictatorship is an authoritarian form of government.

__________ **13.** In a monarchy voters elect a king and a queen.

__________ **14.** A market economy is commonly associated with totalitarianism.

__________ **15.** A country may have a unitary government and a market economy.

__________ **16.** Many rural parts of less developed countries have traditional economies.

__________ **17.** Command economies often exist in democratic countries.

Section 1 Guided Reading and Review

World Resources

A. As You Read

Directions: As you read Section 1, complete the charts below about world resources.

Natural Resources
1. Examples of renewable resources are ____________________________________ .
2. Examples of nonrenewable resources are ____________________________________ .

Energy Sources	
Type	**Drawbacks, if Any**
3. ___________________________	**4.** ___________________________
5. ___________________________	**6.** ___________________________
7. ___________________________	**8.** ___________________________
9. ___________________________	**10.** ___________________________
11. ___________________________	**12.** ___________________________

B. Reviewing Vocabulary

Directions: Complete each sentence by writing the correct term in the blank.

13. People have always used ____________________ , the materials from the natural environment, to help meet their needs.

14. Soil and water are examples of ____________________ .

15. Minerals that cannot be replaced once they are used up are ____________________

____ .

16. Ancient plant and animal remains form ____________________ .

17. ____________________ is produced by splitting uranium atoms.

18. People use ____________________ , or the energy from falling water, to power machines or generate electricity.

19. The earth's internal heat produces ____________________ .

20. Radiation from the sun produces ____________________ .

Section 2 Guided Reading and Review
World Economic Activity

A. As You Read

Directions: As you read Section 2, complete the following charts.

Economic Activities	
Types	**Examples**
Primary	1. _______________________________
Secondary	2. _______________________________
Tertiary	3. _______________________________
Quaternary	4. _______________________________

Economic Development	
Type of Country	**Characteristics**
Developed	5. _______________________________
Underdeveloped	6. _______________________________
Developing	7. _______________________________

B. Reviewing Vocabulary

Directions: Define the following terms.

8. primary economic activity _______________________________

9. subsistence farming _______________________________

10. commercial farming _______________________________

11. secondary economic activity _______________________________

12. cottage industry _______________________________

13. commercial industry _______________________________

14. tertiary economic activity _______________________________

15. quaternary economic activity _______________________________

16. export _______________________________

17. import _______________________________

Regional Atlas Study Guide

The United States and Canada

A. As You Read

Directions: As you work through the Regional Atlas, complete the chart below by writing two supporting details under each main idea.

Main Idea A: The United States and Canada share a number of physical features.

1. ____

2. ____

Main Idea B: Latitude, elevation, and distance from oceans affect the climates of the United States and Canada.

3. ____

4. ____

Main Idea C: The size of the populations of Canada and the United States differs, but in some ways the populations of both nations are similar.

5. ____

6. ____

Main Idea D: Both the United States and Canada have a wide variety of resources and economic activities.

7. ____

8. ____

B. Reviewing Vocabulary

Directions: Define the following terms.

9. colony _______________________________

10. annex _______________________________

11. cede _______________________________

12. civil war _______________________________

13. Industrial Revolution _______________________________

14. continental divide _______________________________

15. drainage basin _______________________________

16. tributary _______________________________

17. striation _______________________________

18. rain shadow _______________________________

19. literacy _______________________________

19. suburb _______________________________

21. standard of living _______________________________

22. per capita _______________________________

Section 1 Guided Reading and Review

A Resource-Rich Nation

A. As You Read

Directions: As you read Section 1, complete the chart below by describing the factors
that have contributed to the economic success of the United States.

Factor	Descriptions
Major natural resources	1. ______________________________ 2. ______________________________ 3. ______________________________

Technological advances
   In water transportation
 	
   In land transportation
 	
   In communication
	4. ______________________________
	______________________________
	
	5. ______________________________
	______________________________
	
	6. ______________________________
	______________________________

American shared values	7. ______________________________ ______________________________
American economic system	8. ______________________________ ______________________________

B. Reviewing Vocabulary

Directions: Define the following terms.

9. gross national product ____

____

10. canal ____

____

11. telecommunication ____

____

12. free enterprise ____

____

Section 2 Guided Reading and Review

A Nation of Cities

A. As You Read

Directions: As you read Section 2, complete the chart below by writing three supporting details under each main idea.

Main Idea A: Changes in transportation affected the growth of American cities.

1. ____

2. ____

3. ____

Main Idea B: Popular preferences and economic activities influence the growth of American cities today.

4. ____

5. ____

6. ____

Main Idea C: American cities can be organized in a hierarchy according to their function.

7. ____

8. ____

9. ____

B. Reviewing Vocabulary

Directions: Define the following terms.

10. metropolitan area ____

11. hierarchy ____

12. hinterland ____

Section 1 Guided Reading and Review

The Northeast

A. As You Read

Directions: As you read Section 1, complete the chart below by writing three supporting details under each main idea.

Main Idea A: The most valuable natural resource of the Northeast is its waters.

1. ____

   ____

2. ____

   ____

3. ____

   ____

Main Idea B: The cities of the Northeast grew in the 1800s and the early 1900s.

4. ____

   ____

5. ____

   ____

6. ____

   ____

B. Reviewing Vocabulary

Directions: Complete the sentence by writing the correct term in the blank.

7. A very large city created when the outer edges of one city reach the outer edges of

   another city is called a ____________________ .

Section 2 Guided Reading and Review

The South

A. As You Read

Directions: As you read Section 2, complete the chart below concerning various characteristics of the South. In the right column, supply effects for each of the causes listed in the left column.

Cause	Effect
Location near the Equator	1. _______________________
Weather systems moving out of the Gulf of Mexico and the Caribbean	2. _______________________
Subtropical climate and rich soils of most of the region	3. _______________________
Rocky soil and steep slopes of Appalachia	4. _______________________
Fast-moving streams of the Piedmont and large oil reserves	5. _______________________
Cheaper land and lower labor costs	6. _______________________
People looking for job opportunities and retirement locations	7. _______________________
Migration of African Americans and Hispanics to the South	8. _______________________

B. Reviewing Vocabulary

Directions: Read the statements below. If a statement is true, write T in the blank. If it is false, write F.

________ 9. A mangrove is a kind of tropical tree that grows in swampy ground along coastal areas.

________ 10. A marshy inlet of a lake or a river is known as a bayou.

________ 11. The fall line is an imaginary line between the Rocky Mountains and the Atlantic coastal plain.

________ 12. The band of southern states stretching from the Carolinas to Texas is called the Sunbelt.

Section 3 Guided Reading and Review

The Midwest

A. As You Read

Directions: As you read Section 3, organize information about Midwest farm products
by completing the chart below.

Place	Crops and Livestock
Warmer, wetter parts of Indiana, Illinois, and Iowa	1. ___________________________________ ___________________________________
Drier Great Plains states	2. ___________________________________ ___________________________________
States such as Wisconsin along the northern margins	3. ___________________________________ ___________________________________

Directions: As you continue to read, write down three supporting details for each main
idea below.

Main Idea A: Farming has changed from a small family enterprise to big business.

4. ____

5. ____

6. ____

Main Idea B: For several reasons, the Midwest has become the home to much
heavy manufacturing.

7. ____

8. ____

9. ____

B. Reviewing Vocabulary

Directions: Read the statements below. If a statement is true, write T in the blank. If it is
false, write F.

__________ **10.** The dark-colored organic material created from the decay of plants and
animals is called humus.

__________ **11.** The growing season is the average amount of rainfall an area receives
from early spring to late fall.

__________ **12.** The place where grain is loaded, cleaned, mixed, and stored is called a grain elevator.

__________ **13.** A grain exchange is a place where buyers and sellers store grain.

Section 4 Guided Reading and Review

The West

A. As You Read

Directions: As you read Section 4, complete the chart below. In the right column, supply a resource, activity, or characteristic described by each sentence in the left column.

Description	Resources, Activities, or Characteristics
The abundance or scarcity of this resource is the major factor affecting the West.	1. ______________________________
Along with uranium, these metals are resources that led to the growth of Western towns.	2. ______________________________
The discovery of this resource transformed the economy of Alaska in the 1960s.	3. ______________________________
This economic activity is important in the Pacific Coast states, as well as Hawaii and Alaska.	4. ______________________________
Nearly half of this comes from the Pacific Northwest.	5. ______________________________
The completion of this promoted the growth of Western cities.	6. ______________________________
Both Hawaii and Alaska are unique among Western states for this reason.	7. ______________________________

B. Reviewing Vocabulary

Directions: Complete the sentence by writing the correct term in the blank.

8. ____________________ is a dry, treeless plain that sprouts grasses and mosses only in

summer when the top layer of soil thaws.

9. A large pipe that carries water over long distances is called a(n)

____________________.

Section 1 Guided Reading and Review

Regions of Canada

A. As You Read

Directions: As you read Section 1, fill in the chart below by providing details about the regions of Canada.

Atlantic Provinces

Names: **1.   2.   3.   4.**

Major landforms/landscapes: **5.** ______________________________________

Economic activities: **6.** ______________________________________

The Great Lakes and St. Lawrence Provinces

Names: **7.   8.**

Major landforms/landscapes: **9.** ______________________________________

10. ______________________________________

11. ______________________________________

Economic activities: **12.** ______________________________________

Prairie Provinces

Names: **13.   14.   15.**

Major landforms/landscapes: **16.** ______________________________________

Economic activities: **17.** ______________________________________

British Columbia and the Northern Territories

Names: **18.   19.**

20. ______________________________   **21.** ______________________________

Major landforms/landscapes: **22.** ______________________________________

23. ______________________________________

Economic activities: **24.** ______________________________________

B. Reviewing Vocabulary

Directions: Define the following terms.

25. province ______________________________________

26. maritime ______________________________________

27. lock ______________________________________

28. bedrock ______________________________________

Section 2 Guided Reading and Review

The Search for a National Identity

A. As You Read

Directions: As you read Section 2, fill in the chart below by supplying the missing information.

Question	Answer(s)
What is the ancestry of the two largest ethnic groups in Canada?	1. ______________________ 2. ______________________
What two groups of people were the first to live in Canada?	3. ______________________ 4. ______________________
Which country surrendered all of its claim to Canadian territory after the British and French wars of the 1700s?	5. ______________________
When did Canada become a completely independent country?	6. ______________________
In which province do most French-speaking Canadians live?	7. ______________________
What are Canada's official languages?	8. ______________________ 9. ______________________
What do the separatists seek?	10. ______________________
From what regions of the world have immigrants most recently been coming to Canada?	11. ______________________

B. Reviewing Vocabulary

Directions: Define the following terms.

12. separatism ____

____

13. secede ____

____

Section 3 Guided Reading and Review

Canada Today

A. As You Read

Directions: As you read Section 3, complete the chart below by writing two supporting details under each main idea.

Main Idea A: Canada faces many challenges with its natural resources and urbanization.

1. ____

____

2. ____

____

Main Idea B: Canada has several important links with the United States.

3. ____

____

4. ____

____

Main Idea C: Canada maintains its links with the world in several ways.

5. ____

____

6. ____

____

B. Reviewing Vocabulary

Directions: Define the following terms.

7. customs ____

____

8. tariff ____

____

9. NAFTA ____

____

Regional Atlas Study Guide

Latin America

A. As You Read

Directions: As you work through the Regional Atlas, complete the chart below by writing two details about each Latin American topic listed.

Physical Characteristics	1. _______________________________ 2. _______________________________
Climates	3. _______________________________ 4. _______________________________
Ecosystems	5. _______________________________ 6. _______________________________
People and Cultures	7. _______________________________ 8. _______________________________
Economics, Technology, and Environment	9. _______________________________ 10. _______________________________
Types of Economic Systems	11. _______________________________ 12. _______________________________

B. Reviewing Vocabulary

Directions: Define the following terms.

13. conquistador _______________________

14. cultural convergence _______________

15. *caudillo* _________________________

16. pampas ____________________________

17. cay ________________________________

18. coral ______________________________

19. tropical storm ______________________

20. hurricane __________________________

21. El Niño ____________________________

22. canopy ____________________________

23. mestizo ____________________________

24. mulatto ____________________________

25. market economy _____________________

26. GDP per capita ______________________

27. command economy _____________________

28. traditional economy __________________

Section 1 Guided Reading and Review
Geography of Mexico

A. As You Read

Directions: As you read Section 1, complete the chart by describing the physical and human features of each region of Mexico.

Region	Physical and Human Features
Central Plateau	**1.** ____
Northern Pacific Coast	**2.** ____
Southern Pacific Coast	**3.** ____
Gulf Coastal Plain	**4.** ____
Yucatán Peninsula	**5.** ____

B. Reviewing Vocabulary

Directions: Define the following terms.

6. plateau ____

____

7. peninsula ____

____

8. irrigation ____

____

9. sinkhole ____

____

Section 2 Guided Reading and Review

A Place of Three Cultures

A. As You Read

Directions: As you read Section 2, answer the following questions.

1. How did Spain make Mexico a colony?

____

____

2. How did Mexico become a democracy?

____

____

3. How has rural life in Mexico changed since 1920?

____

____

4. What are Mexico's major industries? Why?

____

____

B. Reviewing Vocabulary

Directions: Match the definitions in Column I with the terms in Column II. Write the correct letter in each blank.

Column I

__________ **5.** farmland owned collectively by farmers

__________ **6.** commercial farms

__________ **7.** large, Spanish-owned estates of lands run as farms or ranches

__________ **8.** growing only enough crops to meet a family's needs

__________ **9.** people who travel from place to place to do seasonal work on farms

__________ **10.** factories that assemble products almost exclusively for consumers in the United States

__________ **11.** a government policy of breaking up haciendas and distributing the land

__________ **12.** farm produce grown for sale in local or world markets

__________ **13.** a free trade agreement between Canada, the United States, and Mexico

Column II

a. haciendas
b. land redistribution
c. *ejidos*
d. subsistence farming
e. *latifundios*
f. cash crops
g. migrant workers
h. NAFTA
i. *maquiladoras*

Section 1 Guided Reading and Review
Central America

A. As You Read

Directions: As you read Section 1, complete the chart below about Central America by supplying the missing question or answer.

Question	Answer(s)
1. ________________________________	a mountainous core; Caribbean lowlands; the Pacific coastal plain
What are the four main groups of people of Central America?	2. ____________ 3. ____________ 4. ____________ 5. ____________
What classes exist in Central America today?	6. ________________________________
What are the two extremes of Central American farms?	7. ________________________________ 8. ________________________________
9. ________________________________	shortage of farmland; unequal distribution of farmland; favored treatment of the wealthy

B. Reviewing Vocabulary

Directions: Complete each sentence by writing the correct term in the blank.

10. Panama is an ________________________ , a narrow strip of land with water on both sides that connects two larger bodies of land.

11. ________________________ forces are armed units not part of a country's regular army.

Section 2 Guided Reading and Review

The Caribbean Islands

A. As You Read

Directions: As you read about the Caribbean islands in Section 2, fill in the charts below with details for each category listed.

Caribbean Island Groups		
Three Major Groups	**Types of Island Formations**	**Climate of Islands**
1. _______________	4. _______________	7. _______________
2. _______________	5. _______________	
3. _______________	6. _______________	

People of the Islands (non-Europeans)	
8. _______________	9. _______________

Interaction and Movement	
Economic Activities	**Reasons for Migration**
10. _______________	12. _______________
11. _______________	

B. Reviewing Vocabulary

Directions: Complete each sentence by writing the correct term in the blank.

13. The Bahamas are a group of islands, or a(n) _______________ .

14. All of the Bahamas are _______________, islands formed by the remains of tiny, soft-bodied sea animals.

15. The side of the Caribbean islands that *faces* the wind—or the _______________ side—receives heavy rainfall.

16. On the side of the Caribbean islands *away* from the wind—the _______________ side—the amount of rainfall is much less.

The Land and Its Regions

A. As You Read

Directions: As you read Section 1, complete the chart on Brazil's regions by supplying key details on each topic listed.

Regions	Details
The Northeast Region Settlement of the coast	1. ______________________ ______________________
Climate of the *sertao*	2. ______________________
People's lives in the *sertao*	3. ______________________
The Southeast Region Percent of Brazil's land area	4. ______________________
Percent of Brazil's population	5. ______________________
Farming conditions	6. ______________________
Major crops	7. ______________________
Major cities	8. ______________________
Conditions in the cities	9. ______________________
The Brazilian Highlands Location	10. ______________________ ______________________
History of Brasília	11. ______________________ ______________________
The Amazon River Region Percent of Brazil's land area	12. ______________________
Percent of Brazil's population	13. ______________________

B. Reviewing Vocabulary

Directions: Define the following terms.

14. escarpment ____

15. *sertao* ____

16. *favela* ____

Section 2 Guided Reading and Review

Brazil's Quest for Economic Growth

A. As You Read

Directions: As you read Section 2, complete the chart about Brazil's economic development by supplying the missing information.

Question	Answers
What are two major causes of rural poverty in Brazil?	1. _______________________ 2. _______________________
Name three ways the government boosted the growth of industry in Brazil during the 1940s and the 1950s.	3. _______________________ 4. _______________________ 5. _______________________
Name three ways the government encouraged the development of Brazil's interior.	6. _______________________ 7. _______________________ 8. _______________________
Identify three signs of the success of Brazil's development program.	9. _______________________ 10. _______________________ 11. _______________________
Identify two drawbacks to Brazil's development program.	12. _______________________ 13. _______________________

B. Reviewing Vocabulary

Directions: Define the following terms.

14. plantation ____

15. gasohol ____

16. deforestation ____

17. ecotourism ____

____

Section 1 Guided Reading and Review

The Northern Tropics

A. As You Read

Directions: As you read Section 1, complete the chart below to compare the Guianas and Venezuela. Then, answer the questions that follow.

Country	Official Language	Ethnic Background of the Population	Basis of Economy
Guyana	1. ____________	2. ____________ ____________	3. ____________ ____________
Suriname	4. ____________	5. ____________ ____________ ____________	6. ____________ ____________
French Guiana	7. ____________	8. ____________ ____________ ____________	9. ____________ ____________
Venezuela	10. ____________	11. ____________ ____________	12. ____________ ____________

13. How are the landscapes of Venezuela and Colombia alike? ____________________
____

14. On what cash crop does Colombia's economy depend? ____________________
____

B. Reviewing Vocabulary

Directions: Complete each sentence by writing the correct term in the blank.

15. People of mixed African and other ancestry, or ____________ , are a major part of French Guiana's population.

16. ____________ is the mineral used to make aluminum.

17. On either side of Venezuela's Orinoco River lies grassland called the ____________ .

18. In Colombia, the Andes Mountains have three parallel ranges called ____________ .

19. ____________ , or tenant farmers, in Colombia grow coffee but little food.

Section 2 Guided Reading and Review

The Andean Countries

A. As You Read

Directions: As you read Section 2, complete the chart by answering the questions about the Andean countries.

Questions	Answers
Into what three areas do the Andes Mountains divide the Andean countries?	1. _______________________________ 2. _______________________________ 3. _______________________________
What are the two main natural resources of the Andean Highlands?	4. _______________________________ 5. _______________________________
What two groups make up most of the populations of Ecuador and Peru?	6. _______________________________ 7. _______________________________
What group makes up the majority of Chile's population?	8. _______________________________
What products does Chile's Central Valley send to U.S. supermarkets in the winter?	9. _______________________________

B. Reviewing Vocabulary

Directions: Define the following terms.

10. *altiplano* _______________________________

11. *páramo* _______________________________

12. timber line _______________________________

13. *selva* _______________________________

Section 3 Guided Reading and Review

The Southern Grassland Countries

A. As You Read

Directions: As you read Section 3, complete the charts below.

Regions of Southern South America		
Region	**Location**	**Land and/or Climate**
Andean Region	1. _______________	2. _______________
Tropical Lowlands	3. _______________	4. _______________
Grasslands	5. _______________	6. _______________
Patagonia	7. _______________	8. _______________

Countries of Southern South America	
Paraguay Area where most people live	9. _______________
Basis of economy	10. _______________
Uruguay Ethnic background of population	11. _______________
Basis of economy	12. _______________
Argentina Ethnic background of population	13. _______________
Capital city	14. _______________

B. Reviewing Vocabulary

Directions: Match the definitions in Column I with the terms in Column II. Write the correct letter in each blank.

Column I

_________ **15.** cowboys who herded cattle in the pampas

_________ **16.** broad river mouth

_________ **17.** foothills of the Andes

_________ **18.** grasslands of Argentina and Uruguay

Column II

a. estuary
b. piedmont
c. pampas
d. gauchos

Regional Atlas Study Guide

Western Europe

A. As You Read

Directions: As you work through the Regional Atlas, complete the chart below by giving examples of each characteristic of Western Europe.

Centers of Ancient Civilizations	Mountain Ranges
1. _________________________	3. _________________________
2. _________________________	4. _________________________

Peninsulas	Rivers
5. _________________________	9. _________________________
6. _________________________	10. _________________________
7. _________________________	11. _________________________
8. _________________________	12. _________________________

Major Climate Regions	Major Ecosystems
13. _________________________	17. _________________________
14. _________________________	18. _________________________
15. _________________________	19. _________________________
16. _________________________	20. _________________________
	21. _________________________

B. Reviewing Vocabulary

Directions: Complete each sentence by writing the correct term in the blank.

22. Through the process of _________________________ , people adopt the practices of their neighbors.

23. The _________________________ was a period of rebirth and rediscovery of knowledge in Western Europe that began in the 1400s.

24. The growing use of machines in the 1700s and 1800s was the

_________________________ .

25. The _________________________ is the highest point on a mountain.

26. The constant winds that blow from west to east in the earth's temperate zones are the _________________________ .

27. The _________________________ is a single currency used by member nations of the European Union.

28. In Europe and the United States, school is _________________________ , or required, until a certain age.

Guided Reading and Review

Name ___________________________

Date ___________ Class ___________________________

England

A. As You Read

Directions: As you read Section 1, complete the chart below by writing supporting details under each main idea.

Main Idea A: England has three very different geographic regions.

1. Highlands: ____

    ____

2. Midlands: ____

    ____

3. Lowlands: ____

    ____

Main Idea B: London's location has made it one of the most important commercial cities in the world.

4. ____

    ____

5. ____

    ____

Main Idea C: England was once the "workshop of the world," but today it is no longer a leading exporter of manufactured goods.

6. ____

    ____

7. ____

    ____

B. Reviewing Vocabulary

Directions: Match the definitions in Column I with the terms in Column II. Write the correct letter in each blank. You will not use all the terms.

Column I	Column II
________ 8. able to produce abundant crops	a. ore
________ 9. rocky material containing a valuable mineral	b. fertile
________ 10. service industry	c. tertiary economic activity
	d. estuary
	e. euro

Section 2 Guided Reading and Review

Scotland and Wales

A. As You Read

Directions: As you read Section 2, complete the chart below to compare and contrast Scotland and Wales.

Feature	Scotland	Wales
Physical Characteristics	1. ____________________ 2. ____________________	7. ____________________ 8. ____________________
Economy	3. ____________________ 4. ____________________	9. ____________________ 10. ____________________
Culture	5. ____________________ 6. ____________________	11. ____________________ 12. ____________________

B. Reviewing Vocabulary

Directions: Define the following terms.

13. moor ____

14. bog ____

15. glen ____

Section 3 Guided Reading and Review

The Two Irelands

A. As You Read

Directions: As you read Section 3, complete the chart by writing a brief description of each important development in Irish-English history.

Date(s)	Major Developments in Irish-English History
300 B.C.	1. ____
800–1014	2. ____
1066	3. ____
1171	4. ____
1500s	5. ____
1840s	6. ____
1916–1921	7. ____
1949	8. ____
1994	9. ____

B. Reviewing Vocabulary

Directions: Complete each sentence by including a definition of the italicized term.

10. In Ireland, one source of fuel is *peat*, ______________________________

____

____ .

11. Conflict between Irish Protestants and Catholics led to *cultural divergence*, ______________

____

____ .

12. Ireland was devastated in the 1840s by a potato *blight*, ______________________

____

____ .

Section 4 Guided Reading and Review

The Nordic Nations

A. As You Read

Directions: As you read Section 4, complete the chart below to summarize the physical and human characteristics of the Nordic nations.

Feature	Descriptions
Landscape	1. _______________________________________ 2. _______________________________________
Climate	3. _______________________________________ 4. _______________________________________
Culture	5. _______________________________________ 6. _______________________________________
Government and Economy	7. _______________________________________ 8. _______________________________________

B. Reviewing Vocabulary

Directions: Complete each sentence by writing the correct term in the blank.

9. The Scandinavian coast has many steep-walled, deep-water valleys called

   _________________________ , which were formed by glaciers.

10. The people of Iceland have learned to take advantage of the island's geology to

    produce _________________________ .

11. The Nordic nations have _________________________ that include elements of both free
    enterprise and socialism.

Section 1 Guided Reading and Review

France

A. As You Read

Directions: As you read Section 1, complete the chart below by describing the physical features and economy of each region of France.

Region	Physical Geography	Economy
Northern France	1. _______________	2. _______________
Southwestern France	3. _______________	4 _______________
South central and southeastern France	5. _______________	6. _______________
Mediterranean coast	7. _______________	8. _______________
Rhine Valley	9. _______________	10. _______________

B. Reviewing Vocabulary

Directions: Match the definitions in Column I with the terms in Column II. Write the correct letter in each blank

Column I

__________ **11.** regional variations in a language

__________ **12.** style of painting associated with Claude Monet and Pierre Auguste Renoir

__________ **13.** to place a business or industry under government control

__________ **14.** an extended period of little or no economic growth

Column II

a. nationalize
b. Impressionism
c. dialects
d. recession

Section 2 Guided Reading and Review

Germany

A. As You Read

Directions: As you read Section 2, complete the chart below by identifying one or more major results of each event.

Event	Aftermath
Charlemagne's death	1. _________________________________
Protestant Reformation	2. _________________________________
End of Franco-Prussian War	3. _________________________________
End of World War I	4. _________________________________
End of World War II	5. _________________________________
Overthrow of East Germany's government	6. _________________________________

Directions: As you read Section 2, complete the chart below about the regions of Germany.

Region	Physical Features	Economy
Northern	7. _________________	8. _________________
Central	9. _________________	10. _________________
Southern	11. _________________	12. _________________

B. Reviewing Vocabulary

Directions: Define the following terms.

13. confederation ____

14. reparation ____

15. inflation ____

16. lignite ____

Section 3 Guided Reading and Review
The Benelux Countries

A. As You Read

Directions: As you read Section 3, complete the chart below by writing three supporting details under each main idea.

Main Idea A: The Dutch have intensely managed their environment.

1. ____

2. ____

3. ____

Main Idea B: Conflict between two ethnic groups affects Belgian life.

4. ____

5. ____

6. ____

Main Idea C: Luxembourg is a small but prosperous country.

7. ____

8. ____

9. ____

B. Reviewing Vocabulary

Directions: Complete each sentence by writing the correct term in the blank.

10. The Dutch have built _______________________ of earth and rock to hold back the water.

11. The land that the Dutch reclaimed from the sea is called a(n) _______________________ .

12. The Belgian government has passed laws to _______________________ , giving greater authority to the governments in Wallonia, Flanders, and Brussels.

Section 4 Guided Reading and Review

Switzerland and Austria

A. As You Read

Directions: As you read Section 4, complete the charts below.

Switzerland: Facts in Brief

Official languages	1. _______________________
Form of government	2. _______________________
	_______________________
Agricultural exports	3. _______________________
Manufactured products	4. _______________________
	_______________________
Service industries	5. _______________________

Austria: Facts in Brief

Historical highlights	6. _______________________
	_______________________
Industries	7. _______________________
	_______________________
Agriculture	8. _______________________
Mineral resources	9. _______________________
	_______________________
Capital city	10. _______________________

B. Reviewing Vocabulary

Directions: Define the following terms.

11. canton ____

____

12. neutral ____

____

13. perishable good ____________________________________

____

14. strip mining _______________________________________

____

Section 1 Guided Reading and Review
Spain and Portugal

A. As You Read

Directions: As you read Section 1, complete the chart below by writing two supporting details under each main idea.

Main Idea A: The Iberian Peninsula is separated from the rest of Europe by its physical characteristics.

1. ____

2. ____

Main Idea B: Portugal has had great influence overseas during its history.

3. ____

4. ____

Main Idea C: The economies of Spain and Portugal are moving away from agriculture and towards industry.

5. ____

6. ____

B. Reviewing Vocabulary

Directions: Complete each sentence by writing the correct term in the blank.

7. The Guadalquivir is the only Spanish river that is _______________ .

8. Farmers in the Meseta use _______________ methods to grow wheat and barley, leaving the fields unplanted every one or two years to gather moisture.

9. Hot, dry winds from North Africa, called _______________ , create semiarid conditions in southeast Spain.

10. Madrid is Spain's _______________ , a center of economic activity and influence.

Section 2 Guided Reading and Review

Italy

A. As You Read

Directions: As you read Section 2, complete the chart below by listing and describing the major cities in each region of Italy.

Region	Major Cities	Description
Northern Italy	1. ________________ 3. ________________ 5. ________________ 7. ________________	2. ________________ 4. ________________ 6. ________________ 8. ________________
Central Italy	9. ________________ 11. ________________ 13. ________________	10. ________________ 12. ________________ 14. ________________
Southern Italy	15. ________________	16. ________________

B. Reviewing Vocabulary

Directions: Complete each sentence by writing the correct term in the blank.

17. The Apennines Mountains experience a great deal of ____________________ , or many earthquakes and volcanic eruptions.

18. Venice suffers from ____________________ , a geological phenomenon in which the ground in an area sinks.

19. A great period of art and learning called the ____________________ began in Italy in the 1300s and was diffused throughout Europe.

Section 3 Guided Reading and Review
Greece

A. As You Read

Directions: As you read Section 3, organize information about cause and effect in Greece by completing the chart below.

Cause(s)	Effect
1. ________________________ ________________________ 2. ________________________ ________________________ 3. ________________________ ________________________	Greece may be considered part of Mediterranean Europe.
The African and Eurasian tectonic plates meet in southern Greece.	4. ________________________
5. ________________________	Greece has experienced soil erosion.
More than one third of Greece's total population lives in and around Athens.	6. ________________________
7. ________________________	Greece relies heavily on trade over water; shipbuilding is a key industry.
Greece has experienced military conquests by other cultures.	8. ________________________

B. Reviewing Vocabulary

Directions: Complete each sentence by writing the correct term in the blank.

9. The Aegean Sea to the east of the Greek mainland occupies a sunken area of land called a(n) ________________________ .

10. Fewer than 200 of the islands south of Greece are ________________________ , or able to support permanent residents.

11. The giant waves that were once thought to have helped destroy Crete are called ________________________ .

Regional Atlas Study Guide

Central Europe and Northern Eurasia

A. As You Read

Directions: As you work through the Regional Atlas, complete the chart below by writing in details about Central Europe and Northern Eurasia for each topic listed.

Topics	Details
Physical Characteristics	1. _______________________________ 2. _______________________________
Major Climates	3. _______________________________ 4. _______________________________
Major Ecosystems	5. _______________________________ 6. _______________________________
Ethnic Groups	7. _______________________________ 8. _______________________________
Major Economic Activities	9. _______________________________ 10. _______________________________

B. Reviewing Vocabulary

Directions: Define the following terms.

11. domestication _______________________________

12. communism _______________________________

13. Eurasia _______________________________

14. inland sea _______________________________

15. tundra _______________________________

16. taiga _______________________________

17. steppe _______________________________

18. multiethnic _______________________________

19. ethnic group _______________________________

20. acid rain _______________________________

21. infant mortality _______________________________

22. maternal mortality _______________________________

23. life expectancy _______________________________

Section 1 Guided Reading and Review

Poland

A. As You Read

Directions: As you read Section 1, complete the chart below by writing two supporting details under each main idea.

Main Idea A: Poland has varied natural resources.

1. ____

2. ____

Main Idea B: Since World War II, Poland has become a nation composed of one ethnic group.

3. ____

4. ____

Main Idea C: Communists fell from power in Poland because they lacked popular support.

5. ____

6. ____

B. Reviewing Vocabulary

Directions: Complete each sentence by writing the correct term in the blank.

7. Despite centuries of domination by foreign powers, the Polish people maintained their __________________ .

8. The Nazi regime of Germany, after occupying Poland, sealed off the Jewish __________________ within Polish cities.

9. Historians refer to the mass killing of millions of Jews and other Europeans during World War II as the __________________ , a word for a fire that burns something completely.

Section 2 Guided Reading and Review

The Czech and Slovak Republics, and Hungary

A. As You Read

Directions: As you read Section 2, organize information about the Czech Republic, Slovakia, and Hungary by completing the chart below.

Country	Details
The Czech Republic Size Description of Landscape Description of Regions	1. _______________________ 2. _______________________ 3. _______________________
Slovakia Year of Independence Description of Landscape Basis of Economy	4. _______________________ 5. _______________________ 6. _______________________
Hungary Dominant Ethnic Group Main Religion Description of Regions Basis of Economy	7. _______________________ 8. _______________________ 9. _______________________ 10. _______________________

B. Reviewing Vocabulary

Directions: Read the statements below. If a statement is true, write T in the blank. If it is false, write F.

_________ **11.** The Czech rebellion against communism came to be called the "velvet revolution" because it was not harsh enough and eventually failed.

_________ **12.** The Czech government has led a vigorous program of selling state-owned businesses called privatization.

_________ **13.** The Communist regimes of Eastern Europe ended private ownership in agriculture by gathering farmland together in collective farms.

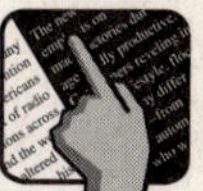

Section 3 Guided Reading and Review
The Balkan Peninsula

A. As You Read

Directions: As you read Section 3, complete the chart below by answering the
questions about the Balkan nations.

Question	Answer
Which country was ruled by a Communist leader named Nicolae Ceausescu, who led the country to economic chaos?	1. ___________________________
Which country is known as the garden of Eastern Europe because of its warm summers and mild winters?	2. ___________________________
Which country, known for decades as "Europe's hermit," is now ending its isolation?	3. ___________________________
Which republics remained joined in the country of Yugoslavia?	4. ___________________________
Which area was the key point of conflict in the late 1990s?	5. ___________________________
Which part of the former Yugoslavia is expected to recover quickly from the problems brought by war and independence?	6. ___________________________
Which country was embroiled in war between three different ethnic groups after declaring its independence?	7. ___________________________
Which country experienced conflict based on its national language policy?	8. ___________________________

B. Reviewing Vocabulary

Directions: Define the following terms.

9. balkanize ____

10. entrepreneur ____

11. multiplier effect ____

Section 4 Guided Reading and Review

Baltic States and Border Nations

A. As You Read

Directions: As you read Section 4, complete the chart below by answering the questions about the Baltic states and border nations.

Question	Answer
Which three nations on the coast of the Baltic Sea were officially republics of the Soviet Union until it broke apart in 1991?	1. _______________________ 2. _______________________ 3. _______________________
The language of which nation is closely related to Finnish?	4. _______________________
Which nation is known as a "breadbasket" of Eastern Europe because of its productive farmland?	5. _______________________
Which nation had more than one fifth of its farmland contaminated by radiation blown across it after the accident at Chernobyl?	6. _______________________
What nation has a population mostly of Romanian descent and continues to have strong ties to Romania?	7. _______________________

B. Reviewing Vocabulary

Directions: Define the following terms.

8. annex ____

9. diversify ____

Section 1 Guided Reading and Review

Regions of Russia

A. As You Read

Directions: As you read Section 1, complete the chart below by writing a supporting detail under each main idea.

Main Idea A: Russia is a large country that contains a variety of physical features.

1. ____

2. ____

Main Idea B: Plant life in Russia is closely related to location and climate.

3. ____

4. ____

Main Idea C: Siberia's geology is complex and presents both problems and wealth.

5. ____

6. ____

B. Reviewing Vocabulary

Directions: Complete each sentence by writing the correct term in the blank.

7. Large areas of central Russia are _____________________ , or broad expanses of rich soil formed by grasslands.

8. Russia's most productive agricultural area has black soil called

   _____________________ .

9. Russia's Arctic shore is dominated by a treeless zone, the _____________________ , containing small plants and animals adapted to polar conditions.

10. The broad forested zone called the _____________________ has trees that do not grow to great size because of harsh conditions.

11. In Siberia, a layer of permanently frozen soil called _____________________ can extend 5,000 feet below the surface.

Section 2 Guided Reading and Review

Emergence of Russia

A. As You Read

Directions: As you read Section 2, answer the following questions.

1. What two groups established the first Russian state in the 800s?

   ____

2. Which Russian czar expanded Russian rule east to the Pacific?

   ____

3. What French ruler invaded Russia in 1812, and why was he forced to retreat?

   ____

4. What 1917 event put an end to rule by czars and established a Communist government?

   ____

5. How did communism affect Russia's economy?

   ____

6. What Soviet leader began radical reforms in the late 1980s?

   ____

B. Reviewing Vocabulary

Directions: Complete each sentence by writing the correct term in the blank.

7. In the past, Russian monarchs were called _____________________.

8. A monarch who gives up his or her crown is said to _____________________.

9. A(n) _____________________ was a governing council of the U.S.S.R.

10. An economy in which a central authority decides what goods will be produced is a(n)

    _____________________.

11. A policy of _____________________, or openness, was instituted in the U.S.S.R. in the late 1980s.

12. In putting _____________________ into effect, the Soviets committed to gradual change to an economic system of private ownership.

Section 3 Guided Reading and Review

Geographic Issues in Russia

A. As You Read

Directions: As you read Section 3, complete the chart below by filling in the correct answers to each question.

Question	Answer
What are three leisure activities Russians may enjoy?	1. _______________________________ 2. _______________________________ 3. _______________________________
Identify the republic in the Caucasus region where intense fighting recently occurred when it tried to gain independence from Russia.	4. _______________________________
What is Russia's major means of transportation?	5. _______________________________
What are three problems that the transition from a command economy to a market economy has caused Russia?	6. _______________________________ 7. _______________________________ 8. _______________________________
Identify two bodies of water in or around Russia with major pollution problems.	9. _______________________________ 10. _______________________________

B. Reviewing Vocabulary

Directions: Complete each sentence by writing the correct term in the blank.

11. The official Russian currency, the ____________________ , had an official value of U.S. $1.75, but lost value after the fall of communism.

12. The ____________________ , or an informal transfer of goods and services without official record keeping, has grown in Russian in response to economic instability.

Regional Atlas Study Guide

Central and Southwest Asia

A. As You Read

Directions: As you work through the Regional Atlas, complete the chart below. Under each main idea, write two or three supporting details.

Main Idea A: Central and Southwest Asia is the birthplace of three of the world's major religions.

1. ____

2. ____

3. ____

Main Idea B: Much of the land in Central and Southwest Asia is dry.

4. ____

5. ____

Main Idea C: The countries in this region have found ways to compensate for a short supply of fresh water.

6. ____

7. ____

B. Reviewing Vocabulary

Directions: Define the following terms.

8. agricultural revolution ____

9. civilization ____

10. monotheism ____

11. protectorate ____

12. chaparral ____

13. poaching ____

14. mosque ____

15. muezzin ____

16. minaret ____

17. desalination plant ____

18. nomad ____

19. trade deficit ____

20. trade surplus ____

Section 1 Guided Reading and Review
The Caucasus Nations

A. As You Read

Directions: As you read Section 1, complete the chart below about the Caucasus nations by supplying the missing question or answer.

Question	Answer(s)
What are the names of the Caucasus nations?	1. ______________________________ 2. ______________________________ 3. ______________________________
4. _______________________________	Black Sea and Caspian Sea
Which two nations have had recent conflicts due to religious tensions?	5. ______________________________ 6. ______________________________
Which two Caucasus nations are not landlocked?	7. ______________________________ 8. ______________________________
9. _______________________________	They are predominantly Islamic.
Which nation's major source of wealth is oil?	10. ______________________________
Which country's subtropical climate allows growth of wine grapes, citrus fruit, and tea?	11. ______________________________

B. Reviewing Vocabulary

Directions: Complete each sentence by writing the correct term in the blank.

12. Several ethnic groups in Georgia have pressed for more _______________________ , or independence.

13. _______________________ is the systematical killing or intentional destruction of a people.

14. The desire of the Azeri and Armenian cultural groups to rule themselves in separate nations is called _______________________ .

Section 2 Guided Reading and Review

The Central Asian Nations

A. As You Read

Directions: As you read Section 2, fill in the chart on Central Asia below with details for each category listed.

<table>
<tr><td colspan="4" align="center">Central Asia</td></tr>
<tr><td colspan="2">Nations</td><td colspan="2">Largest Deserts</td></tr>
<tr><td>1. ______________</td><td>4. ______________</td><td colspan="2">6. ______________________________</td></tr>
<tr><td>2. ______________</td><td>5. ______________</td><td colspan="2">7. ______________________________</td></tr>
<tr><td>3. ______________</td><td></td><td colspan="2"></td></tr>
<tr><td colspan="2">Rural Economic Activities</td><td colspan="2">Major Environmental Problems</td></tr>
<tr><td colspan="2">8. ______________________________</td><td colspan="2">10. ______________________________</td></tr>
<tr><td colspan="2">9. ______________________________</td><td colspan="2">11. ______________________________</td></tr>
</table>

B. Reviewing Vocabulary

Directions: Complete each sentence by writing the correct term in the blank.

12. ______________________ is a rich topsoil that is good for agriculture.

13. ______________________ , a set of religious beliefs based on a strict interpretation of a sacred text, is common in many parts of Central Asia.

14. Traditional herders in Central Asia often lived in ______________________ , large, portable, round tents made of wooden frames covered with felt or skins.

15. The diversion of water from the Aral Sea has caused ______________________ , the extension of the desert landscape due to changes caused by humans.

Section 1 Guided Reading and Review
Creating the Modern Middle East

A. As You Read

Directions: As you read Section 1, complete the chart below by writing two supporting details under each main idea.

Main Idea A: World War I had a great impact on the Middle East.

1. ____

____

2. ____

____

Main Idea B: Both Arabs and Jews had historical ties to Palestine.

3. ____

____

4. ____

____

Main Idea C: In 1947, the British government turned over the problem of
Palestine to the United Nations.

5. ____

____

6. ____

____

B. Reviewing Vocabulary

Directions: Complete each sentence by writing the correct term in the blank.

7. A(n) _______________________ was land to be governed on behalf of the League of
Nations until it was ready for independence.

8. A(n) _______________________ is a member of a movement founded to promote the
establishment of an independent Jewish state in Palestine.

9. Arabs in Palestine were angered when they thought the British took away their

right of _______________________ .

Section 2 Guided Reading and Review

Israel

A. As You Read

Directions: As you read Section 2, complete the chart below to summarize the development of Israel.

Technology Transforms the Desert	Mining the Dead Sea
1. ______________________ ______________________ 2. ______________________ ______________________	3. ______________________ ______________________ 4. ______________________ ______________________
Economic Activities	**Diverse Cultures**
5. ______________________ ______________________ 6. ______________________ ______________________	7. ______________________ ______________________ 8. ______________________ ______________________
Palestinian Refugees	**The Struggle for a Solution**
9. ______________________ ______________________ 10. ______________________ ______________________	11. ______________________ ______________________ 12. ______________________ ______________________

B. Reviewing Vocabulary

Directions: Define the following terms.

13. drip irrigation

____

____

14. potash

____

____

Section 3 Guided Reading and Review
Jordan, Lebanon, Syria, and Iraq

A. As You Read

Directions: As you read Section 3, answer the following questions.

1. What was the impact of the 1967 Arab-Israeli War on Jordan's economy?

2. What kind of government does Jordan have? _______

3. When did Lebanon become independent from France? _______

4. According to the 1932 census, which religious group held the most power in Lebanon?

5. What was the major reason behind Lebanon's civil wars?

6. Why did Israel invade Lebanon in 1982?

7. What activity has been carried on for centuries in the Syrian cities of Damascus and Aleppo?

8. What measures has the Syrian government taken to enhance farm production in Syria?

9. What is Iraq's most important economic activity?

10. In what ways has Iraq used its oil profits?

11. From 1980 to 1988, Iraq was engaged in a war with which other Southwest Asian country?

12. What was the outcome of the Persian Gulf War for Iraq?

B. Reviewing Vocabulary

Directions: Read the following definitions. Then write the correct term on each blank.

_______ 13. an arc of rich land in the Middle East where farming and the first civilizations developed

_______ 14. a private army of a particular fighting faction

_______ 15. a state of lawlessness, political disorder, and violence

_______ 16. a restriction on trade with other countries

Section 4 Guided Reading and Review

Arabian Peninsula

A. As You Read

Directions: As you read Section 4, complete the chart below by writing two supporting details under each main idea.

Main Idea A: Discovery of oil in the 1930s greatly changed traditional ways of life in the Arabian Peninsula.

1. ____

   ____

2. ____

   ____

Main Idea B: Many changes have occurred in Saudi Arabia since the mid-1960s.

3. ____

   ____

4. ____

   ____

Main Idea C: Oman and Yemen are different from other countries on the Arabian Peninsula.

5. ____

   ____

6. ____

   ____

B. Reviewing Vocabulary

Directions: Match the definitions in Column I with the terms in Column II. Write the correct letter in each blank.

Column I

__________ 7. process of removing salt from seawater so that it can be used for drinking and irrigation

__________ 8. a country's basic support facilities, such as roads, schools, and communication systems

__________ 9. an ancient system of underground and surface canals in Oman

Column II

a. *falaj* system
b. desalination
c. infrastructure

Section 5 Guided Reading and Review

Turkey, Iran, and Cyprus

A. As You Read

Directions: As you read Section 5, answer the following questions.

1. What kind of language and culture did the Turks have?

   ____

2. What are three changes that Mustafa Kemal brought to Turkey?

   ____

   ____

   ____

3. What are two challenges that face Turkey today?

   ____

   ____

4. What are two major changes that Shah Mohammad Reza Pahlavi brought to Iran?

   ____

   ____

5. What are two major social changes that the Khomeini government brought to
   Iranian society?

   ____

   ____

6. To what branch of Islam do the majority of Iranians belong?

   ____

7. What is the chief language spoken in Cyprus?

   ____

8. Which two groups are involved in the civil war in Cyprus?

   ____

   ____

B. Reviewing Vocabulary

Directions: Define the following terms.

9. secular ____

10. shah ____

11. ayatollah ____

Regional Atlas Study Guide

Africa

A. As You Read

Directions: As you work through the Regional Atlas, complete the chart below by supplying an effect for each cause listed.

Cause-and-Effect Relationships	
Cause	**Effect**
European countries divided Africa without regard to existing political and cultural divisions.	**1.** ____________________________ ____________________________
Many of Africa's rivers have waterfalls.	**2.** ____________________________ ____________________________
People in Africa clear rain forest areas for farming, grazing, and lumbering.	**3.** ____________________________ ____________________________
Poverty is widespread in many rural areas of Africa.	**4.** ____________________________ ____________________________

B. Reviewing Vocabulary

Directions: Complete each sentence by writing the correct term in the blank.

5. The region just south of the Sahara is the ____________________ .

6. ____________________ is a system in which a foreign power controls a nation and exploits its resources and markets.

7. A(n) ____________________ is an elevated block of land with a flat or gently rolling surface.

8. A(n) ____________________ is a steep slope or cliff.

9. Drought-resistant brush is called ____________________ .

10. A(n) ____________________ is a grassland with scattered trees.

11. Africa has a tradition of ____________________ , or history passed down by word of mouth.

12. In ____________________ , herders move flocks to different pastures throughout the year.

13. The dissolving and washing away of nutrients in soil is ____________________ .

14. The reduction in the productive potential of land is ____________________ .

15. The ____________________ of a country is the average number of people in a given unit of area.

Guided Reading and Review

Section 1 Guided Reading and Review

Egypt

A. As You Read

Directions: As you read Section 1, complete each sentence in the boxes below to provide details about Egypt.

Egypt and Its People

1. Most of the population lives _______________________.

2. Desert regions lie _______________________.

3. Many rural people migrate to the cities for _______________________

   _______________________.

4. Today, Egyptian farmers are both helped and hindered by _______________________

   _______________________.

The Economy

5. Egypt's economy is strained by its _______________________.

6. Egypt's main exports now are _______________________ , but Egypt

   needs a(n) _______________________ to ensure its economic stability.

7. Industrial development has been limited by a lack of _______________________

   and _______________________ .

B. Reviewing Vocabulary

Directions: Complete each sentence by writing the correct term in the blank.

8. A(n) _______________ is land formed by soil in the water that is dropped as a river slows and enters the sea.

9. Egyptian peasants are called the _______________ .

10. The *khamsin* creates _______________ that blow hot air, dust, and grit into the Nile Valley.

11. A(n) _______________ is a traditional Arab open-air market.

12. Trapping floodwaters by building walls around fields is called _______________ .

13. A(n) _______________ is an artificial lake behind a dam.

14. A system for providing additional water to crops year-round is _______________ .

15. _______________ is money invested in building and supporting new industry.

Section 2 Guided Reading and Review

Libya and the Maghreb

A. As You Read

Directions: As you read Section 2, complete the charts below to summarize the way of life in North African nations.

The People of North Africa
Effect of Location on Culture
1. ____
Population of North Africa
2. ____
Rural Life
3. ____
Nomadic Life
4. ____
Urban Life
5. ____

North Africa Today
Libyan Economy and Government
6. ____
7. ____
Algerian Economy and Government
8. ____
9. ____
Tunisian and Moroccan Economy
10. ____

B. Reviewing Vocabulary

Directions: Complete each sentence by writing the correct term in the blank.

11. Dry riverbeds and sharp gullies, or _______________________, cut across the North African desert.

12. Merchants joined together in _______________________ to cross the desert in safety.

13. The older Arab sections of North African cities, called _______________________, are usually centered around mosques.

14. North African markets are called _______________________.

Guided Reading and Review

Section 1 Guided Reading and Review
The Sahel

A. As You Read

Directions: As you read Section 1, complete the chart below with information about the rich and varied history of the Sahel.

Dates	History of the Sahel
5000 B.C.	1. _______________________________________
A.D. 400 to 1076	2. _______________________________________
1300 to 1600	3. _______________________________________
The present	4. _______________________________________
The future: three goals	5. _______________________________________ 6. _______________________________________ 7. _______________________________________

B. Reviewing Vocabulary

Directions: Complete each sentence by writing the correct term in the blank.

8. Moving crops to new soil every couple of years is called _______________________.

9. Food for grazing animals is called _______________________.

10. _______________________ strips land of its trees.

11. The land's loss of all vegetation is called _______________________.

12. A person fleeing home to live elsewhere and escape danger or unfair treatment is

    a(n) _______________________.

13. A country is _______________________ when it has no seaport.

14. A(n) _______________________ is an area of lakes, creeks, and swamps away from the ocean.

<table>
<tr><td>Name</td><td></td></tr>
<tr><td>Date</td><td>Class</td></tr>
</table>

Section 2 Guided Reading and Review

The Coastal Countries

A. As You Read

Directions: As you read Section 2, complete the chart below by writing two supporting details under each main idea.

Main Idea A: Because of their location near the sea, the coastal countries of West Africa have a long history of trade with foreign nations.

1. ____

____

____

2. ____

____

____

Main Idea B: Since gaining independence, both the government and the people of West Africa are struggling to improve economic conditions.

3. ____

____

4. ____

____

Main Idea C: The cultures of West Africa still reflect many traditional roles and beliefs.

5. ____

____

6. ____

____

B. Reviewing Vocabulary

Directions: Complete each sentence by writing the correct term in the blank.

7. A(n) _____________________ is a sudden political takeover.

8. The idea that the spirits of the dead will live on if the people still living continue to honor and respect them is the basis of _____________________ .

9. The belief that gods or spirits can be found in ordinary things such as the sky and trees is called _____________________ .

Section 3 Guided Reading and Review

Nigeria

A. As You Read

Directions: As you read Section 3, complete the chart below to organize information about influences on Nigerian history.

Cause	Effect
Nigeria is a land of both good and poor soil.	1. ________________________________
Nigeria's people come from many different groups.	2. ________________________________
In Nigeria in the early 1980s, the sale of oil provided most of the country's income.	3. ________________________________
The World Bank imposed a structural adjustment program.	4. ________________________________
General Abacha declared elections void and seized power.	5. ________________________________

B. Reviewing Vocabulary

Directions: Define the following terms.

6. World Bank

____

____

7. International Monetary Fund

____

____

8. structural adjustment program

____

____

Section 4 Guided Reading and Review

Central Africa

A. As You Read

Directions: As you read Section 4, complete the chart below with examples of the movement of people in Central Africa.

Movement in Central Africa	
Methods of moving people and goods	1. ______________________________ ______________________________ 2. ______________________________ ______________________________
Barriers to movement	3. ______________________________ ______________________________ 4. ______________________________ ______________________________
Direction of movement	5. ______________________________ ______________________________
Effect of movement	6. ______________________________ ______________________________

Directions: As you read Section 4, fill in two examples of the interaction between the people of Central Africa and their environment.

7. ______________________________

____

8. ______________________________

____

B. Reviewing Vocabulary

Directions: Complete each sentence by writing the correct term in the blank.

9. A(n) ________________ is a central ridge dividing two river basins.

10. Fighting that involved foreign troops, rebel armies, and ________________ has plagued the Democratic Republic of the Congo for four years.

11. When people don't use money, they may exchange goods through ________________ .

  Guided Reading and Review

Section 1 Guided Reading and Review

Kenya

A. As You Read

Directions: As you read Section 1, answer the following questions.

1. Where is Kenya located?

____

2. Where do most Kenyans live?

____

3. Describe the land and climate of the highlands.

____

____

4. What two groups occupied the central highlands in the 1890s?

____

5. How did the British affect the development of Kenya?

____

____

6. What group of people fought against the British in the Mau Mau Rebellion?

____

____

7. How did *harambee* affect Kenya after independence?

____

____

____

8. Why do many Kenyans suffer from malnutrition?

____

____

B. Reviewing Vocabulary

Directions: Define the following terms.

9. *harambee* ____

10. pyrethrum ____

11. malnutrition ____

Section 2 Guided Reading and Review

Other Countries of East Africa

A. As You Read

Directions: As you read Section 2, complete the chart by identifying the correct East African nations.

Other Countries of East Africa	
Which four countries have strategic value because of their location on the Horn of Africa?	1. ______________________________ 2. ______________________________ 3. ______________________________ 4. ______________________________
Which country is the largest in area in all of Africa?	5. ______________________________
Which four countries of East Africa are landlocked?	6. ______________________________ 7. ______________________________ 8. ______________________________ 9. ______________________________
Which two countries of East Africa are ethnocracies?	10. ______________________________ 11. ______________________________
In which East African country did the economy turn around after socialism ended?	12. ______________________________

B. Reviewing Vocabulary

Directions: Complete each sentence by writing the correct term in the blank.

13. The value of a country's location for nations planning large-scale military action is

    called its ___________________ .

14. A form of government in which one ethnic group rules over others is a(n)

    ___________________ .

15. Forcing rural people to move into towns and work on collective farms is called

    ___________________ .

Section 3 Guided Reading and Review

South Africa

A. As You Read

Directions: As you read Section 3, complete the chart below by writing three supporting details under each main idea.

Main Idea A: A white minority controlled South Africa for many years.

1. ____

2. ____

3. ____

Main Idea B: To control black South Africans, the South African government established homelands and apartheid.

4. ____

5. ____

6. ____

Main Idea C: External and internal pressures forced the South African government to end apartheid and move toward majority rule.

7. ____

8. ____

9. ____

B. Reviewing Vocabulary

Directions: Complete each sentence by writing the correct term in the blank.

10. A system of laws instituted in South Africa to keep black Africans and whites apart

　　was called _______________________ .

11. Forced separation of racial groups is called _______________________ .

12. _______________________ are actions that punish a country for behavior unacceptable
　　to the international community of nations.

Section 4 Guided Reading and Review

Other Countries of Southern Africa

A. As You Read

Directions: As you read Section 4, complete the chart by identifying the correct southern African nations.

Question	Answer(s)
Which two countries are completely or almost completely surrounded by and dependent on South Africa?	1. __________________ 2. __________________
Which country until recently was almost a colony of South Africa?	3. __________________
Which landlocked country of southern Africa has attracted a large population because of its fertile land and excellent water supply?	4. __________________
In which landlocked, arid country does the relatively small population benefit from the sale of diamonds, copper, coal, and beef cattle?	5. __________________
Which two countries were once Portuguese colonies, suffered from white flight after achieving independence, and established Communist economic systems?	6. __________________ 7. __________________
Which country became poor after relying on copper as a source of revenue and allowing agriculture to decline?	8. __________________
Which country kept agriculture productive by pursuing a gradual land redistribution program after independence?	9. __________________

B. Reviewing Vocabulary

Directions: Define the following terms.

10. enclave ____

11. white flight ____

12. land redistribution ____

Regional Atlas Study Guide
South Asia

A. As You Read

Directions: As you work through the Regional Atlas, complete the chart below by identifying each of the South Asian features or characteristics listed.

Features or Characteristics	Descriptions	
Early Civilizations and States of South Asia	1. _______________ 2. _______________	3. _______________
Countries of South Asia	4. _______________ 5. _______________ 6. _______________ 7. _______________	8. _______________ 9. _______________ 10. _______________
Major Cities of South Asia	11. _______________ 12. _______________	13. _______________
Major Mountain Ranges of South Asia	14. _______________	15. _______________
Major Religions of South Asia	16. _______________ 17. _______________	18. _______________

B. Reviewing Vocabulary

Directions: Define the following terms.

19. sultanate

____

20. nonaligned nation

____

21. subcontinent

____

22. alluvial plain

____

23. monsoon

____

Section 1 Guided Reading and Review

Road to Independence

A. As You Read

Directions: As you read Section 1, answer the following questions.

1. Why was India's textile industry almost completely destroyed?

   ____

2. What Western ideas were spread among the Indian middle class in the late 1800s?

   ____

3. What was Gandhi's most powerful weapon against the British?

   ____

4. In what way did Gandhi use nonviolent resistance to show opposition to the sale of British cloth?

   ____

5. What happened to the sale of British cloth in India as a result of Gandhi's actions?

   ____

6. What decision did the British government make in 1935?

   ____

7. What was the basis of the partition of the Indian subcontinent in 1947?

   ____

8. What results did the 1947 independence of India and Pakistan have on their inhabitants?

   ____

9. What problems arose between the regions of West Pakistan and East Pakistan, and what was the result?

   ____

   ____

B. Reviewing Vocabulary

Directions: Complete each sentence by writing the correct term in the blank.

10. A strong sense of _______________________ , or pride in one's nation, developed in India during the late 1800s.

11. _______________________ is the policy of opposing an enemy or oppressor by any means other than violence.

12. To _______________________ a product or service is to refuse to purchase, sell, or use it.

13. To _______________________ a nation is to divide it into parts.

Section 2 Guided Reading and Review
India's People and Economy

A. As You Read

Directions: As you read Section 2, complete the chart below by writing three supporting details under each main idea.

Main Idea A: The caste system involves a social hierarchy.

1. ____

2. ____

3. ____

Main Idea B: People in rural Indian villages follow a traditional way of life.

4. ____

5. ____

6. ____

Main Idea C: India is one of the leading industrial nations in the world.

7. ____

8. ____

9. ____

B. Reviewing Vocabulary

Directions: Define the following terms.

10. reincarnation ____

11. caste system ____

12. charpoy ____

13. sari ____

14. purdah ____

15. joint family system ____

16. cottage industry ____

Section 3 Guided Reading and Review

Other Countries of South Asia

A. As You Read

Directions: As you read Section 3, organize information about other countries of South Asia by completing the chart below.

Country	Physical and Other Features
Pakistan	1. ______________________________
	2. ______________________________
Afghanistan	3. ______________________________
	4. ______________________________
Bangladesh	5. ______________________________
	6. ______________________________
Nepal and Bhutan	7. ______________________________
	8. ______________________________
Sri Lanka	9. ______________________________
	10. ______________________________

B. Reviewing Vocabulary

Directions: Define the following terms.

11. hydroelectric power ______________________________

12. irrigate ______________________________

13. embankment dam ______________________________

14. buffer state ______________________________

15. malnutrition ______________________________

16. deforestation ______________________________

Regional Atlas Study Guide

East Asia and the Pacific World

A. As You Read

Directions: As you work through the Regional Atlas, complete the chart below by writing at least one supporting detail under each main idea.

Main Idea A: Some of humanity's earliest technological advances occurred in East and Southeast Asia.

1. ____

____

Main Idea B: The collision of the Eurasian and Indian tectonic plates has altered the geography of East and Southeast Asia.

2. ____

____

Main Idea C: Seasonal rainfall affects parts of East Asia, Southeast Asia, Australia, and New Zealand in a variety of ways.

3. ____

____

Main Idea D: East Asia and the Pacific region have many different ecosystems.

4. ____

____

Main Idea E: Much of the world's population lives in East and Southeast Asia.

5. ____

____

Main Idea F: Many factors explain great differences in transportation systems among the countries of China, Japan, Australia, and Thailand.

6. ____

____

B. Reviewing Vocabulary

Directions: Define the following terms.

7. concession ____

8. intensive farming ____

9. terrace ____

10. bullet train ____

Section 1 Guided Reading and Review

The Emergence of Modern China

A. As You Read

Directions: As you read Section 1, complete the chart below to organize information about China, by writing supporting details under each idea.

Main Idea A: In the 1920s, a split developed in the Nationalist party.

1. ____
   ____

2. ____
   ____

Main Idea B: Mao Zedong's economic and political reforms did not succeed.

3. ____
   ____

4. ____
   ____

Main Idea C: The Four Modernizations gave a boost to China's economy.

5. ____
   ____

6. ____
   ____

B. Reviewing Vocabulary

Directions: Complete each sentence by writing the correct term in the blank.

7. An area controlled by a country but not directly governed by it is called

   a(n)________________________ .

8. To ________________ is to give up a throne.

9. In China, a(n) ________________________ was a regional leader with an army.

10. The production of small consumer goods is usually referred to as

    ________________________ .

11. In May of 1989, the Chinese government imposed ________________________ in China.

Section 2 Guided Reading and Review
Regions of China

A. As You Read
Directions: As you read Section 2, answer the following questions.

1. In the past few decades, what region of China has become the center of its booming economy? _______________________________

2. What color is the loess soil? _______________________________

3. Why is the Huang He also called China's Sorrow? _______________________________

4. What is the purpose of terrace farming along the slopes of hills?

5. What river serves as China's east-west highway?

6. Three of the four Special Economic Zones are located in which province of China?

7. What is the chief economic activity in Northwest China?

8. What physical feature dominates the Southwest region?

9. What religion is the Tibetan society based on?

10. What was the result of the Tibetan uprising of 1959?

B. Reviewing Vocabulary
Directions: Complete each sentence by writing the correct term in the blank.

11. Growing more than one crop a year on the same land is called _______________________________ .

12. A(n) _______________________________ is someone who claims to rule by religious or divine authority.

13. A political unit with limited self-government is known as a(n) _______________________________ .

Section 3 Guided Reading and Review

China's People and Culture

A. As You Read

Directions: As you read Section 3, complete the chart below to organize information about China by writing two supporting details under each main idea.

Main Idea A: China's one-couple, one child population policy has had differing effects in different parts of China.

1. ____

2. ____

Main Idea B: China is a land of great ethnic diversity.

3. ____

4. ____

Main Idea C: Written Chinese is different from many other written languages.

5. ____

6. ____

Main Idea D: Officially, China is an atheist country, but religious belief is not absent.

7. ____

8. ____

B. Reviewing Vocabulary

Directions: Complete each sentence by writing the correct term in the blank.

9. Pictures or characters that represent a thing or an idea are called

______________________ .

10. ______________________ is the denial of the existence of God.

11. The Chinese use ______________________ , which is the practice of inserting needles into the body to cure diseases or ease pain.

Section 4 Guided Reading and Review
China's Neighbors

A. As You Read

Directions: As you read Section 4, complete the chart below by writing a brief description of each topic listed.

Topic	Description
China's neighbors	**1.** _______________________________________
Nationalist migration	**2.** _______________________________________
Taiwanese industries	**3.** _______________________________________
Hong Kong	**4.** _______________________________________
Mongols	**5.** _______________________________________

Directions: Use the chart above and your textbook to answer questions 6–10.

6. Which of China's neighboring countries is also an island? _______________________

7. Who was the leader of the Nationalists? _______________________

8. On what kind of industries has Taiwan concentrated recently? _______________________

9. When did Hong Kong become part of China again? _______________________

10. Politically, has Mongolia been influenced more by China or Russia? _______________________

B. Reviewing Vocabulary

Directions: Define the following terms.

11. buffer _______________________________________

12. provisional government _______________________________________

13. exodus _______________________________________

Section 1 Guided Reading and Review

Japan: The Land of the Rising Sun

A. As You Read

Directions: As you read Section 1, complete the chart below by writing a brief description of each feature of Japan.

Feature	Description
Landform	1. ________________________________
Landscape	2. ________________________________
Tectonic activity	3. ________________________________
Influences on climate	4. ________________________________
	5. ________________________________
	6. ________________________________
Population density	7. ________________________________
Ethnic makeup	8. ________________________________
Religious influences	9. ________________________________

B. Reviewing Vocabulary

Directions: Complete each sentence by writing the correct term in the blank.

10. A(n) __________________ is a device that detects movements in the earth's crust.

11. Tropical hurricanes that bring heavy rains to Japan in late summer and early fall are

    called __________________ .

12. Japan's population is considered to be __________________ , because 99 percent
    of the people share the same cultural background.

Section 2 Guided Reading and Review
Japan's Economic Development

A. As You Read

Directions: As you read Section 2, complete the chart below by supplying an effect for each cause listed.

Cause	Effect
Japan's government feared that early European traders might take over their country. (1639)	1. ________________________
Commodore Perry used a show of force to negotiate a trade agreement between the United States and Japan. (1853)	2. ________________________
The new Meiji government decided to strengthen Japan so it would no longer be at the mercy of foreign powers. (1868-1912)	3. ________________________
Japan's lack of natural resources was an obstacle to industrialization. (1900-1937)	4. ________________________
In World War II, Japan fought on the side of Nazi Germany and was defeated. (1939-1945)	5. ________________________
The Japanese obtained raw materials through trade and worked to improve efficiency and quality in manufacturing. (1945-1960s)	6. ________________________

B. Reviewing Vocabulary

Directions: Define the following terms.

7. militarism ____

8. downsizing ____

9. tariffs ____

10. quotas ____

Section 3 Guided Reading and Review

The Koreas: A Divided Peninsula

A. As You Read

Directions: As you read Section 3, complete the charts below to summarize the similarities and differences between North and South Korea.

Similarity	North and South Korea
Culture	1.
Religion	2.

Difference	North Korea	South Korea
Government	3.	4.
Climate	5.	6.
Land and resources	7.	8.
Economy today	9.	10.

B. Reviewing Vocabulary

Directions: Define the following terms.

11. demilitarized zone

12. proliferation

Section 1 Guided Reading and Review

Historical Influences on Southeast Asia

A. As You Read

Directions: As you read Section 1, organize information about the different cultural influences on Southeast Asia by completing the chart below. For each culture, list the appropriate historical events and the impact of that culture's interaction with Southeast Asia.

Culture	History and Impact
Indian	**1.** History _______________________________ **2.** Impact _______________________________
Muslim	**3.** History _______________________________ **4.** Impact _______________________________
Chinese	**5.** History _______________________________ **6.** Impact _______________________________
European	**7.** History _______________________________ **8.** Impact _______________________________

B. Reviewing Vocabulary

Directions: Define the following terms.

9. barbarians _______________________________

10. paddy _______________________________

11. indigenous _______________________________

Section 2 Guided Reading and Review

The Countries of Southeast Asia

A. As You Read

Directions: As you read Section 2, complete the chart about the countries of Southeast Asia by writing supporting details under each main idea.

Main Idea A: Several factors have contributed to Myanmar's weak economy.

1. ____

2. ____

Main Idea B: Although Thailand's economy was once dependent on agriculture, it is now diversified.

3. ____

4. ____

5. ____

Main Idea C: Although Vietnam, Laos, and Cambodia are ethnically different, they have much in common.

6. ____

7. ____

8. ____

Main Idea D: Singapore's success has much to do with its physical features and location.

9. ____

10. ____

B. Reviewing Vocabulary

Directions: Define the following terms.

11. insurgent ____

____

12. *doi moi* ____

____

13. heterogeneity ____

____

Section 1 Guided Reading and Review

Australia

A. As You Read

Directions: As you read Section 1, complete the chart below with the names of Australia's major cities and one feature that makes each one unique.

Australia's Major Cities	
City	**Unique Feature**
1.	2.
3.	4.
5.	6.
7.	8.
9.	10.
11.	12.
13.	14.
15.	16.

Directions: In the space provided, write the correct answer to each question.

17. What obligation did the Aborigines pass down in their myths about the Dreamtime?

____

____

18. What are three major economic activities in Australia today?

____

B. Reviewing Vocabulary

Directions: Complete each sentence by writing the correct term in the blank.

19. The first Australians, the ___________________ , probably crossed a land bridge from Southeast Asia to Australia about 50,000 years ago.

20. A(n) ___________________ is a shallow body of water with an outlet to the ocean.

21. Darwin, Australia, has twice been leveled by ___________________ .

22. The harsh wilderness region of the central and western plains and plateaus in Australia is called the ___________________ .

23. Ranchers provide their sheep and cattle herds with water from ___________________ bored deep in the earth.

Section 2 Guided Reading and Review

New Zealand and the Pacific Islands

A. As You Read

Directions: As you read about New Zealand in Section 2, complete the chart below with a brief description of each feature listed.

Topography	Original People	Land
1. ________________ ________________ ________________ ________________	2. ________________ ________________ ________________ ________________	3. ________________ ________________ ________________ ________________
Climate	**Economy**	**Major Cities**
4. ________________ ________________ ________________ ________________	5. ________________ ________________ ________________ ________________	6. ________________ ________________ ________________ ________________

Directions: As you read about the Pacific Islands in Section 2, fill in the blanks in the following sentences.

7. The two main types of Pacific Islands are ___________________________
____.

8. The three groups of the Pacific Islands are ___________________________
____.

9. Tourism is an important activity in the Pacific Islands because it ___________
____.

10. Two examples of economic activity in the Pacific Islands that are not related to tourism are
____.

11. Most islands achieved independence in the ______________________________.

B. Reviewing Vocabulary

Directions: Define the following terms.

12. geyser ____

13. atoll ____

14. trust territory ____

Section 3 Guided Reading and Review
Antarctica

A. As You Read

Directions: As you read Section 3, organize information about Antarctica's ice by filling in the charts below.

The Effect of Antarctic Ice	
On the continent's elevation	1.
On the land surface	2.
On the Antarctic climate	3.

Types of Ice Formations		
	Location	**Characteristics**
Ice sheets	4.	5.
Glaciers	6.	7.
Ice shelves	8.	9.
Pack ice	10.	11.

B. Reviewing Vocabulary

Directions: Complete each sentence by writing the correct term in the blank.

12. A large crack in a glacier is a(n) _______________________ .

13. Ice that extends out over the ocean is a(n) _______________________ .

14. _______________________ is a mix of icebergs and other floating ice.

15. A(n) _______________________ is a spot where Antarctic waters meet warmer waters.

16. _______________________ are shrimplike creatures in Antarctic waters.